Contents

At Night

HOUGHTON MIFFLIN   BOSTON

Printed in China

ISBN-13: 973-0-618-93256-6
ISBN-10: 0-618-93256-9

1 2 3 4 5 6 7 8 9 SDP 15 14 13 12 11 10 09 08

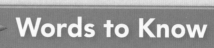

Words to Know

bright   high

Dwight   light

flashlight   night

heart

2

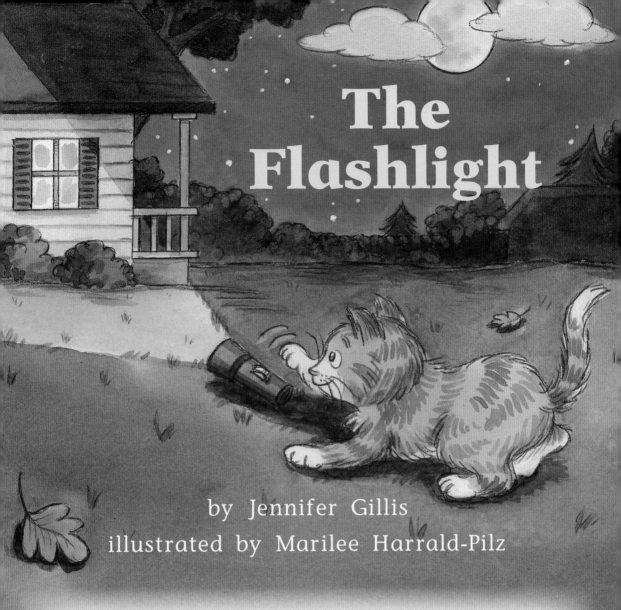

The Flashlight

by Jennifer Gillis

illustrated by Marilee Harrald-Pilz

This is Clue. She is out in the garden at night. She finds a small flashlight on the ground. The light is very bright.

The flashlight lights up the dark
yard. Clue sees a blue sneaker and
a broom. She sees the moon high in
the sky.

Now the flashlight shines on the tool shed. An owl is on the roof. It swoops down over Clue.

The owl hoots, but Clue doesn't mind. She has a happy heart. She likes to see the owl. She climbs high in the tree to see it.

Dwight is in his bedroom. He
looks high and low. He cannot find
his flashlight. He cannot find his
cat, Clue. All of a sudden, he sees
a light in the yard. "What is that?"
he thinks.

"Mom!" said Dwight. "I see a light outside!"

Dwight and his mom go out to the yard. What do they find?

lie	lighthouse
bright	lightning
flashlight	lights
high	night

alphabet   heart

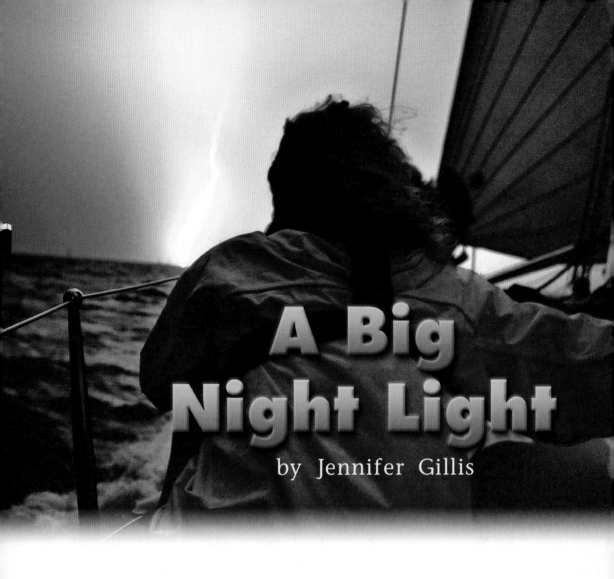

A Big Night Light

by Jennifer Gillis

A ship is at sea. It is not far from the shore. It is in the heart of a storm. What can help the ship see the shore? A lighthouse!

If you go to the beach, you might see a lighthouse. You cannot see the light shine during the day. A lighthouse shines at night. It is like a huge flashlight that you can see for miles.

The light in a lighthouse is at the top. It is very bright! It can shine through rain and fog. It shows ships where sharp rocks lie in the water.

Lighthouses reach high into the sky. To get to the room where the light is, you have to climb many stairs. People don't mind the long climb up.

There is a lighthouse for almost every letter of the alphabet. This one is called Nubble Light. Many people go to see it in Maine.

Some lighthouses are very old, and some are new. Lighthouses still help ships at sea.